Copyright © 2023 Alina Daria

All rights reserved.

ISBN: 9798397299626

Contents

Introduction and systematics

Snakes are becoming increasingly popular as pets, and corn snakes are the undisputed frontrunners in domestic terrariums! But why is that? Well, the corn snake is one of the calmer and more frugal snake species. It is also non-poisonous. Compared to other snake species, the Corn snake is quite easy to keep, making it a good choice for any beginner who would like to keep a snake. However, even though corn snakes are particularly suitable for amateurs, you must of course make an effort to provide the snakes with a home that is as species appropriate as possible. In this guide, we will discuss how exactly this can be done!

The scientific name of the corn snake is "Pantherophis guttatus", established by the Swedish naturalist Carl von Linné (LINNAEUS) in 1766. There is only one species of corn snake as a pet, which is widely kept and sometimes called the 'common corn snake' - however, through selective breeding, there are now many different variants or morphs, which differ in colour, for example. Therefore, there is sometimes a misconception that there are different species of the common corn snake - all common corn snakes belong to the same species, but there are different breeding forms.

However, it should be mentioned that besides the common corn snakes there are also the special prairie corn snakes (Pantherophis emoryi), which are also a species of their own, but are much less commonly kept as pets. While the Pantherophis guttatus inhabits numerous terrariums in many countries of the world as a popular pet, it is rarely found in domestic terrariums. Therefore, we will only deal with the common corn snake.

Animal species are assigned to animal genera - this is, so to speak, the upper category for all animal species that are represented in the respective genus. Corn snakes belong to the genus Pantherophis. This genus is not monotypic, i.e., it does not have only one species, but the genus also includes ground snakes and fox snakes. They are naturally assigned to the family of colubrids (Colubroidea).

As a rule, common corn snakes reach a length of about 100 to 150 centimetres. There are, of course, slightly larger and slightly smaller specimens, but the norm is between one and one and a half metres. As pets, corn snakes can even reach an age of twenty years - wild animals usually do not live as long as captive snakes due to external hazards, lack of health care, etc. This fascinating reptile is also known as the "corn snake".

This fascinating reptile is a loner - corn snakes do not live in groups or lose associations like many other species but rely only on themselves. They are very cosy snakes that spend a lot of time relaxing in their hiding places and usually show little potential for aggression. This also makes them popular pets.

As Corn snakes are solitary animals in the wild, I recommend keeping them alone in the terrarium as well, in order to recreate the natural living conditions as best as possible. However, it is also possible to keep several corn snakes together in a large terrarium if there are enough hiding places so that the animals can always avoid each other. Otherwise, the animals can become aggressive.

Especially for beginners, I find it more advisable to get only one corn snake at first to avoid possible problems.

By Kapa65 Karsten Paulick

The Corn Snake's Home

Common corn snakes (hereafter referred to as "corn snakes") are native to North America. They can be found in the United States of America as well as in Mexico and Canada.

In the wild, corn snakes are usually found during the day, as they are diurnal animals. They usually hunt early in the morning or late in the afternoon to avoid having to hunt in too much heat. Their daily rhythm is similar to that of humans, as corn snakes also sleep or rest at night and protect themselves from predators in their hiding places. For example, they use hollow tree trunks, underground caves or large stones under which there is space to hide.

Since corn snakes want to avoid too high temperatures when hunting, as already mentioned, it is also possible that they become nocturnal during particularly hot summer days and actually hunt at night because it is too hot during the day.

In winter, Corn snakes go into what is known as brumation - this means that they do not sleep soundly, but instead extremely lower their metabolism and "freeze". During this time, energy is saved, and the animal also uses the break for regeneration. Many other reptile species also hibernate, especially reptiles in Europe, to escape food shortages in winter.

In North America, corn snakes inhabit meadows and forests as well as deserts and swamps! Even in the wild, different colour variations of corn snakes can be found - mainly red, yellow, brown and orange - but more unusual variations have resulted from selective breeding.

Corn snakes do not only live on the ground - oh no, not at all! They are extremely good swimmers and climbers. Therefore, they can not only move in the water, but also climb trees and rocks.

Our Corn snakes that are kept as pets are usually offspring - that is, the offspring of snakes that have been caught in the wild. The offspring are not familiar with life in the wild. Although corn snakes do not belong to the endangered species, only offspring should be purchased so that the animals are not taken away from their home and their life in the wild.

Corn snakes are carnivores and feed on a variety of small animals in the wild - they can feed on small mammals and birds as well as other reptiles and amphibians. However, corn snakes have been observed to focus on rats and mice when hunting.

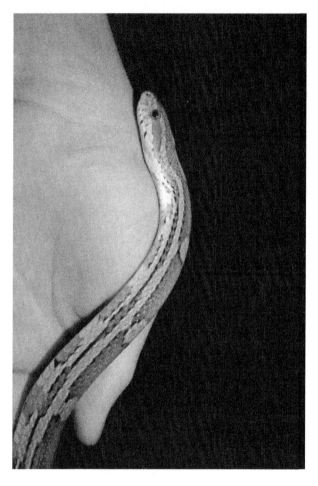

By Kapa65 Karsten Paulick

Feeding

It is part of a corn snake's instincts to hunt down its food and eat it alive. However, this is prohibited in many countries of the world and in some countries, for example, only already dead mice may be fed to snakes. Feeding live vertebrates - which includes mice and rats - has been banned by law in Germany, for example, and is enshrined in the Federal Animal Protection Act.

This was confirmed by a ruling of the Administrative Court of Munich in 2016, because vertebrates such as mice and rats that are intended to be fed to snakes, for example, must be properly killed under anaesthesia beforehand. This is based on paragraph 1 of the Animal Protection Act, which states that no one may inflict pain, suffering or harm on an animal without reasonable cause.

So, snakes should be used to or accustomed to accepting already dead animals as food instead of live food.

Adult corn snakes are fed approximately every seven to ten days. Baby corn snakes need a little more food to grow and are therefore fed every five to seven days.

A frequently asked question deals with the amount of food - the feeding intervals are now clear, but how much food does the snake need? Well, this depends on the size and weight of the snake in question. The food should make up about ten to fifteen percent of the body weight of the respective corn snake. This usually corresponds to one to two food animals.

Pinky mice are suitable for young corn snakes, as they are not too big. Pinky mice can also be used for adult corn snakes, possibly more than one depending on the weight.

It is also important that the food animals themselves were healthy, because if the food animals were sick and, for example, were infested with parasites, these will naturally be passed on to the corn snake when it is fed. This should be prevented by always ensuring that the feed animals are of impeccable quality and that the seller has a good reputation.

Those who cannot feed mice or rats to their corn snake for ethical or other reasons have the option of switching to other foods. In the wild, corn snakes feed mainly on mice and rats, so they are also the best food in the home terrarium, because we want to reproduce the natural living conditions as well as possible, of course. However, if no mice or rats are fed, many keepers resort to feeding insects such as crickets, grasshoppers, zophobas worms and the like. These can be fed frozen (thawed), dried or alive, because unlike vertebrates, invertebrates can be fed to snakes in a living state. This also allows them to follow their natural hunting instinct.

It is advisable to leave the corn snake alone for about one to two days after feeding, because if they are picked up shortly after feeding, for example, it is possible that they will vomit up the last meal again, as digestion is not complete or advanced.

Of course, the snake should always have access to fresh water. There should be a drinking bowl with fresh water in the terrarium, which is always kept clean. Some keepers also use a very large bowl so that the corn snake can lie down in the water instead of just drinking. This is not necessary, but many corn snakes will gladly take a bath. Even if the owner never or very rarely sees the snake drinking, fresh water should always be available.

Corn snakes are pure carnivores, so additional feeding of vegetables or similar is not necessary. Feeding animal protein provides the snake with everything it needs to live. Some keepers also feed quail or fish, for example. This sometimes also depends on the respective region.

If you do not want to feed animal food for ethical reasons, you should get another pet instead of a corn snake - there are also herbivorous reptiles that can be kept well in a terrarium. Corn snakes cannot digest plant food as their digestive system is not designed for this. Since they are not able to extract the necessary nutrients from plant food and excrete them virtually unused, corn snakes should be fed animal food, because - even if it is not easy for many people - only this type of diet is species-appropriate for corn snakes.

If corn snakes are fed an unbalanced diet that is not species-appropriate, there is a high risk of malnutrition. Species-unfriendly snakes are more susceptible to disease and their immune systems are often weakened. This applies to all species; every animal should be fed a species-appropriate, balanced and healthy diet, whether carnivorous, herbivorous or omnivorous.

By Silvia Sipa

The Terrarium

Keeping a corn snake in a terrarium in a species-appropriate manner requires special attention to the temperature and humidity in the corn snake's home. As corn snakes are cold-blooded animals, they cannot regulate their body temperature themselves, but depend on the ambient temperature and adapt to it.

A hot spot of about 30 degrees Celsius, created for example by a 75-watt heat lamp, is important to ensure sufficient heat supply. However, hot spots are not used in some countries. The lighting duration should be between 12-14 hours daily.

Some keepers also use heat mats, which are attached to the outside of the terrarium and heat only one side of the terrarium, in order to achieve slightly different temperatures in the terrarium.

In the rest of the terrarium, the temperature should be between 20-25 degrees Celsius, at night preferably below 20 degrees Celsius, for example at 18 degrees Celsius, so that an artificial day-night rhythm is created. Thermal insulation with polystyrene can help to keep the temperature in the terrarium constant.

The terrarium should have a minimum size of 100x50x50 cm, for two corn snakes the size should be 150x100x100 cm, as recommended by the German Animal Welfare Association. The humidity in the terrarium should be between 40 and 60 percent. To increase the humidity, the terrarium can be sprayed, or an automatic humidifier can be used. The German Animal Welfare Association recommends a humidity of between 50 and 60 percent. It is usually sufficient to humidify the terrarium with a fine spray bottle from time to time. Large puddles should not occur.

Easy-to-clean and non-toxic materials such as newspaper, cardboard, beechwood chips, coconut fibre substrate or peat-free potting soil with fine pine bark are recommended as substrate. Leaves can also be scattered on top. The German Animal Welfare Association recommends a sand-soil-loam mixture. The soil should be loose and absorbent, germ-free and free of fertiliser additives. Good heat conduction and burrowing ability are also advantageous, as corn snakes like to dig.

Real branches of deciduous trees or a few plants in the terrarium offer Corn snakes climbing opportunities and hiding places. It is important that the branches are free of resin and thorns. Large stones, roots, cork and stone tubes or clay serve as hiding places. It is advisable

at least one elevated vantage point using

in the terrarium. Branches and rough
stones can also help with moulting to rub off
excess skin residue if the old skin does not fall off
on its own in some places.

A water dish in the terrarium is essential to
maintain moisture levels and provide the snake
with a place to bathe and drink. The water should
always be fresh and replaced regularly.

A thorough cleaning once a month is
recommended, including changing the floor and
disinfecting the fixtures, to ensure a hygienic
environment for the Corn snake. Vinegar water,
for example, is sufficient for disinfection because
it has an antibacterial effect but is of course free of
chemicals.

Afterwards, it should be wiped with clear water and the snake should not come into contact with vinegar.

By Silvia Sipa

Ten common diseases

Everyone gets sick sometimes. Some more often, others less often. Even reptiles like corn snakes are not immune to diseases and the severity ranges from "mild" to "potentially fatal". But how often and how severely a corn snake falls ill can be determined to a large extent. As with humans, prevention is key - a corn snake that is kept in a species-appropriate manner, whose needs are met and which receives a balanced and healthy diet, is very unlikely to become ill. Of course, certain diseases can occur even if an animal is kept in perfect conditions, for example through heredity or just plain bad luck. However, over 90% of diseases in reptiles are caused by humans - not intentionally, but mostly through simple ignorance of the optimal husbandry conditions.

Among the most common mistakes regarding husbandry and nutrition are, for example ...

... too much dryness in the terrarium (always keep an eye on the humidity)

... overfeeding (many species in "captivity" often gratefully accept everything that humans provide and often no longer regulate themselves)

... stress (e.g., due to lack of space)

... fear (e.g., due to too few hiding places)

... temperatures that are too high or too low.

It is not always necessary to visit the vet for every little problem. A visit to the vet is always stressful, because the corn snake is torn away from its familiar environment and has to face a very stressful and exhausting situation, which can sometimes even take several hours, including the journey.

Nevertheless, for liability reasons, I will not recommend self-treatment or self-medication. Especially beginners may misjudge and treat diseases incorrectly, as they do not have much experience with corn snakes. I therefore point out that diseases must always be identified and professionally treated by a competent veterinarian.

When choosing a vet, make sure that the person chosen has experience with reptiles. This is an absolute must. Reptiles are so fundamentally different from other pets such as rodents, dogs, cats, etc. that a reptile cannot be treated by just any veterinarian. A reputable vet will only treat a Corn snake anyway if they feel confident to do so based on their experience and can treat the animal professionally.

In some areas it can be quite difficult to find a vet who is well versed in reptiles.

This varies from region to region. It is possible that a fairly long journey will have to be accepted. A long journey is of course more stressful for the animal, but it is better than having the animal treated by a vet who does not know reptiles well and may make mistakes. Therefore, it is a good idea to start looking for a suitable vet at an early stage in order to have the right contact person at hand immediately in case of an emergency.

Of course, the owner must be sensitised to the recognition of diseases. If you know your animals, you will notice quite quickly if something is wrong and if an animal changes. Not every little change has to be a sign of a disease, but the following signs often indicate diseases - especially if they occur in a combination ...

... loss of appetite, refusal of food

... sudden aggressiveness and irritability; or the opposite: sudden lethargy / apathy

... unnatural movements

... changes in excretions (faeces and urine) in terms of shape, colour and/or consistency

... loss of joy of movement

... discolouration or detachment of the skin.

Although a disease is a case for the vet, the owner should be able to recognise the different diseases in principle. Therefore, we will now take a closer look at ten common corn snake diseases.

1. aeromonads

Aeromonads are bacteria that can cause diseases in reptiles such as corn snakes. These bacteria are usually found in stagnant water. They nest in the animal's digestive tract and often cause infections. Symptoms include loss of appetite, diarrhoea, dehydration and lethargy. Therefore, drinking and bathing water should be changed regularly, and care should always be taken to ensure good water quality. Still water from the bottle is good. The rest of the environment should also be kept clean at all times to avoid contaminating the water.

2. flagellates

Flagellates are protozoa that can cause infections in reptiles such as corn snakes. Protozoa are tiny organisms that consist of only one cell and perform all the functions necessary for their survival within that one cell.

If a corn snake has a flagellate infection, typical symptoms include diarrhoea, weight loss and dehydration, but these symptoms also occur in a variety of other diseases.

The route of transmission of protozoa is varied and they can be passed on, for example, through feed, contaminated water or direct contact with infected animals.

3. cocci

Unfortunately, cocci infections are quite common in corn snakes. They are single-celled micro-organisms that are often found in the gut of snakes and can have serious consequences for the health of a sick animal. Although they are usually found in the gut, they can also grow outside the gut and cause infection elsewhere.

But what triggers a cocci infection? Well, the possible triggers are manifold and include, for example, (too much) stress, poor hygienic conditions in the terrarium, an inadequate diet that is not species-appropriate, a weak immune system or similar.

At the beginning of a coccus infection, loss of appetite with weight loss, diarrhoea or dehydration can often be observed. A weaker condition is also one of the symptoms. If the disease is not treated but continues to progress, there are often changes in the skin and/or respiratory problems. The earlier the infection is detected, the better it is, of course. A competent veterinarian will decide what treatment is appropriate for the progress of the disease - for example, antibiotics may also be used.

Of course, it is also necessary to find out what triggered the infection. For example, a corn snake may be very stressed if it has to share a small terrarium with another corn snake and the two have little opportunity to get out of each other's way due to lack of space. Non-species food can also cause infection, so it is always best to base animal feeding on the diet of the species in the wild.

4. cryptosporidiosis

Unfortunately, cryptosporidiosis is also quite common in corn snakes. Cryptosporidiosis is caused by a protozoan that attacks the intestinal wall of the snake causing weight loss, diarrhoea and dehydration. A protozoan is a single-celled organism that is usually found in soil or water and belongs to the eukaryotes - this particular protozoan is called cryptosporidium.

The diarrhoea that occurs can be mild or severe. Blood and/or mucus may be found in the faeces. It is absolutely necessary to have cryptosporidiosis treated by a competent veterinarian, because if left untreated, the disease can, in the worst case, lead to the death of the animal or permanently weaken the immune system. In most cases, the administration of antibiotics is necessary, but the veterinarian will determine the specific treatment plan.

Of particular note is the fact that cryptosporidiosis can also be transmitted to humans! Diseases that can pass from animals to humans are called zoonotic diseases. Transmission occurs through direct contact with infected animals, for example, if you pick up your snake that has contracted cryptosporidiosis without gloves, but also through the consumption of contaminated food or water.

Therefore, sick animals should be handled with gloves for safety.

5. mouth rot

Mouth rot occurs in many different reptile species and also in fish. In corn snakes it is quite common, and the disease is caused by the bacterium "Aeromonas hydrophila".

Foot rot is so named because it can cause sores and ulcers in the animal's mouth, affecting the palate as well as the tongue and gums.

Foot rot is best recognised by swollen, red and/or bleeding areas in or around the mouth. These affected areas may continue to be covered by a white layer.

Again, a competent veterinarian will treat this condition with antibiotics in most cases.

6. mites

Mites are parasites that - unlike worms, for example - do not live inside the animal but on the skin. Therefore, they can often be seen from the outside, but this is not always the case. The more severe the infestation, the more likely it is that even a layperson can recognise a mite infestation. Mites like to nest in "corners", so they mainly infest the cloaca, the corners of the mouth, but also eyes, nostrils and similar parts of the body. Mites cause itching, so affected snakes usually rub themselves on objects to relieve the itch. The stronger the immune system, the better the animals cope with mites. If the immune system is not particularly good anyway, for example due to an unhealthy diet or stress, the animal suffers particularly badly from the infestation. As a rule, a mite infestation must be treated with appropriate medication, which the expert veterinarian will prescribe. It is also important to clean the terrarium thoroughly and replace the substrate to avoid a new infestation after treatment.

7. paramyxo viruses

Paramyxo viruses are a dangerous viral strain that can cause a severe disease in a corn snake, also known as stomatitis-pneumonia complex.

The disease is usually recognised by symptoms such as weight loss, shortness of breath, inflammation of the eyes or discharge from the nose. Diseased animals can suffer from inflammation of the mouth, eyes and especially the respiratory tract. The viruses are usually transmitted through direct contact with infected animals, but also via contaminated objects.

8. salmonella

The bacterial infection Salmonella can also occur in corn snakes and the transmission routes are diverse. For example, Salmonella bacteria can be found in the eggs of snakes or can be transmitted through contaminated water and food. Transmission through other objects is also possible.

Symptoms vary and include diarrhoea, weight loss, loss of appetite, lethargy and the like.

Salmonella can also be transmitted to humans, so it is also a zoonotic disease. If an animal is suspected of having the disease, it should always be handled with gloves.

The weaker the immune system, the more serious a Salmonella infection can be. A weak immune system is promoted, for example, by too much stress, by a diet that is not appropriate for the species, by a lack of hygiene and the like. In humans, children and older people in particular have a weaker immune system, so they should be kept away from sick animals.

Regular cleaning and disinfection as well as regular changing of drinking and bathing water for the snake prevents Salmonella infection and other diseases - prevention is always good and limits the risk of disease, but never excludes it completely.

9. scale rot

Scale rot, as the name suggests, affects the scales and skin of the corn snake. The disease is quite widespread and is caused by a fungus. This fungus is the Ophidiomyces ophiodiicola.

If a corn snake is affected by scale rot, this is usually recognised by a loss of scales, general changes in the texture of the skin, but also by ulcers, redness and/or swelling, for example. If the disease is not treated, there is a risk that it will spread over the entire body of the snake.

Like many of the aforementioned diseases, scale rot is caused, for example, by a lack of hygiene, an unfamiliar diet and/or too much stress, all of which weaken the immune system, but a common cause is also moisture disorders. This is another reason why you should always make sure that the humidity in the terrarium is sufficiently high, but not too high, as this can also lead to problems. A humidity of between 40% and 60% is to be aimed for.

10. worms

Worms are widespread parasites that infest all kinds of animals and of which there are many different varieties. In corn snakes, for example, hookworms and roundworms are common and are a burden on the digestive system.

But how does a corn snake become infected with worms? Well, mostly the transmission takes place through the consumption of infected mice or rats. But it is also possible for other animals, such as a second corn snake, to infect the animal. This is another reason why it is essential to pay close attention to where you get the food for your snake.

If a corn snake is infested with worms, it often suffers from weakness, diarrhoea and weight loss. However, these symptoms are also common with other diseases. A competent vet will be able to examine the diseased snake and determine an accurate diagnosis including treatment options.

Some keepers also have their snake wormed as a precaution, but this is usually not necessary, although it is not harmful either. Whether preventive deworming is advisable is a matter of controversy.

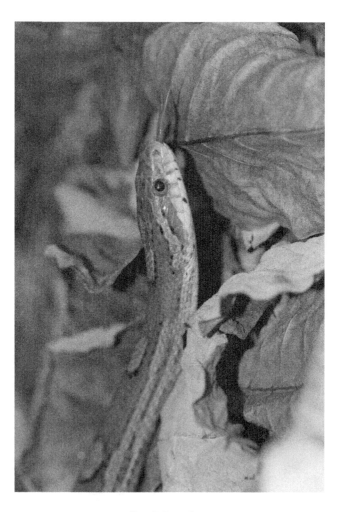

By Silvia Sipa

Buying the Corn snake

If one wants to acquire pets, many people almost automatically turn to a conventional pet shop. However, pet shops unfortunately often give the wrong advice, as the staff are often not specially trained in reptiles. This is not only the case with reptiles such as corn snakes, but also with other popular pets such as rodents, amphibians, fish and co. Therefore, it is advisable to at least take the information from pet shops with a grain of salt.

Furthermore, pet shops often sell animals that are not ready to be given away - some animals are injured, some animals are sick, some animals are still too young. It will usually be difficult for a layperson to judge whether an animal is ready to be given away.

Therefore, it is more advisable to buy reptiles like corn snakes from a reputable breeder. Reputable breeders either concentrate on one specific species of Corn snakes or on only a few different species of Corn snakes. This allows them to gain a lot of experience and they are experts in their respective field. At the time of delivery, the animals must be healthy, must not show any injuries and must be old enough. It is not necessary for a Corn snake to be fully grown when it is surrendered, but it must at least have reached its surrender weight.

A reputable breeder will pay attention to all these points and give comprehensive advice to the new owner. Serious breeders attach great importance to their animals being placed in beautiful and species-appropriate homes and are therefore happy to answer any open questions. The animal will also be prepared for transport.

The price of a Corn snake varies but it cannot be named in a general way. The price depends on the age of the snake as well as on its colouring, because the more unusual and rarer the breeding form, the higher the value. Especially the latter can be decisive for the price.

Depending on the age and colour variety of the corn snake, the price per animal can range from 10 to 500 euros or even higher. Sometimes you can also get animals from animal shelters.

There are basically four ways to acquire a corn snake.

The first option is to buy from a reputable breeder. Usually, breeders devote a lot of time and love to raising their charges, so a good breeder will also be happy to give comprehensive advice to a beginner. It is advisable to look at everything carefully before buying a corn snake from a breeder to get an insight into the rearing conditions.

Corn snakes can also be found or ordered in specialist terrarium shops and larger pet shops. However, this option should only be chosen if there is no breeder available nearby. Although you can see how the animals are kept on site, you still lack insight into the breeding process. This is a clear disadvantage of buying a corn snake in pet shops.

Buying at an animal exchange is even more critical. Here you have even less insight into the keeping and breeding of the corn snakes. It is especially difficult for beginners to recognise diseases and poor husbandry in an animal. Nevertheless, fairs are interesting because you can find many different colour varieties there. They offer an overview and serve for further education.

In any case, before buying, one should intensively study the keeping and breeding conditions of the respective breeder. It should be examined whether the animals are kept in a species-appropriate manner, whether they have enough space, what the rearing conditions are like and whether everything is hygienic. Furthermore, the breeder should be asked about the course of the last moult of the animal you are interested in.

Of course, it is also possible to get corn snakes from a reptile care centre or second hand. Most reptile centres are privately owned, but animal shelters also have corn snakes from time to time. Taking a second-hand corn snake because it is no longer wanted in its old home is also a commendable decision. However, there is a risk of unintentionally taking on a sick animal that would be better off in expert hands until it is healthy again.

By Silvia Sipa

Behaviour

The behaviours of reptiles in general and snakes in particular are sometimes very different from the behaviours of other animals or humans. Therefore, many gestures are often misinterpreted. The following is a brief overview of common behaviours of a corn snake to avoid misinterpretation in the future and to interpret the behaviour correctly.

Vibrating tail tip:

In stressful situations, corn snakes may vibrate violently with the tip of their tail. This vibration produces a rattling sound, which is supposed to scare off the opponent. This behaviour is especially common in young animals. However, if the snake is not exposed to stress, it does not rattle its tail. If the behaviour is observed, it is a sign that something is wrong with the way the snake is housed (for example, two corn snakes in too small a space).

Rearing and biting:

The Corn snake straightens the front third of the body. This usually happens in the so-called S-position, which is typical for many snake species. If the threat persists, the snake lunges forward, performing defensive bites to send the opponent fleeing.

Flight:

The Corn snake feels threatened and decides not to fight but to flee the situation.

Climbing:

In the terrarium there should definitely be some climbing possibilities (e.g., larger deciduous tree branches from the forest), because corn snakes are very good climbers. Although they live mainly on the ground - mostly hidden - they often climb in the wild. During their climbing tours, they capture birds as food, for example, or they raid the birds' nests. This is not done in the home terrarium, of course, but nevertheless the snakes enjoy some opportunities to climb.

Tongues:

Corn snakes have an excellent olfactory organ, but they smell in a different way than we humans do, for example: Corn snakes lick, just like most snakes. By licking, they pick up the scents of their surroundings and can use them to recognise prey, for example. But how does this work? Well, when the tongue is retracted after licking, the snake guides the tip of its tongue down the throat to its so-called Jacobson's organ. This is the olfactory organ, which is also found in other animal species.

The Jacobson's organ is an essential part of the chemical sensory system of corn snakes and enables them not only to find food animals, but also to detect potential mates and to explore the environment. This organ is located in the roof of the Corn snake's mouth and consists of paired mucous membrane pockets. Pheromones can also be sensed by the Jacobson's organ.

Moulting:

All reptiles shed their skin, including our corn snakes. By regularly shedding the old layer of skin, the Corn snake can make room for further growth. Furthermore, moulting also serves to remove possible damage and skin infections. The moult is very important for regeneration. For the moult to be successful, it is important that the humidity in the terrarium is neither too high nor too low - 40 to 60 percent is appropriate. If the skin does not come off in some places, some reptiles like to scrape it off on stones, for example, so it is advisable to also have a large stone in the terrarium.

Young snakes shed their skin about eight to twelve times a year. Adult snakes grow more slowly, so they shed their skin less often.

Experience shows that shortly before moulting, the colour of the skin becomes paler and the eyes take on a slightly milky colour and become a little cloudy. Then it is best to give the snake a lot of rest and not to disturb it. Corn snakes often also become less active just before moulting.

No movement:

If the snake does not move and the tongue is also still in the mouth, there is a high chance that the snake is sleeping. This is not easy to determine because snakes do not have eyelids that they could close to sleep. So, they always have open eyes, even when sleeping. You should not make any frantic movements and approach the terrarium calmly.

Hissing:

Hissing is not a positive sound. The snake wants an opponent to move away. Sometimes snakes also hiss when they simply want to have their peace and quiet so that the human moves away.

Musking/ defecating while holding the snake:

The Corn snake perceives you as a predator and tries to escape with droppings or an unpleasant smelling musk.

Clouded / bluish eyes:

The snake is preparing to molt. It can be particularly defensive because it cannot see well, so you should be all the more careful with it.

By Silvia Sipa

When can corn snakes start reproducing?

Corn snakes can reproduce from about two to three years of age. However, they will only reproduce if they have gone into brumation beforehand.

What is brumation?

Brumation is not true hibernation. The animal does not sleep deeply but reduces its bodily functions and its metabolism slows down drastically. During this time, the snake recovers and the body has time to regenerate.

Usually, brumation begins in nature from around mid-December. During brumation, the animal is not fed. In addition, the temperature in the terrarium is lowered to about 20 degrees Celsius.

In addition, the lighting is not used for as long. While other species (such as the Greek tortoise) have to spend their brumation in special boxes, sometimes even in refrigerators, the corn snake can spend its brumation quietly in the terrarium as long as it is no longer fed, the temperature is lowered, and the lighting time is drastically reduced.

The brumation period lasts about six to eight weeks. After brumation, corn snakes shed their skin quite quickly.

Where does the name "Corn snake" come from?

Well, the origin of the name "corn snake" in these snakes is linked to the popular crop maize, but two different explanations exist. The first is that the name was chosen because of the corn-like pattern on their belly. The second theory is that humans often found this species near cornfields because they liked to hunt mice and rats there. Maize is called "corn" in English.

Do corn snakes only live in the USA?

Actually, yes. Corn snakes originated in the USA, but the illegal trade has spread all over the world. Corn snakes have also been discovered in Australia and captured by animal welfare organisations. Although Australia and the USA are different continents, the Australian habitats are suitable for corn snakes. However, no large population has yet been established in Australia. The snakes that have been found have either escaped or been deliberately released. If this continues, Australia could be faced with a new invasive snake species.

Have Corn snakes established themselves in other countries?

Corn snakes have not only established in Australia, but also on several Caribbean islands because people brought them from the USA and released them into the wild. There are already permanent populations of corn snakes in the Bahamas, the US Virgin Islands and Grand Cayman. When travelling with corn snakes, you must be aware of snake transport laws, as the introduction of a new species into an ecosystem can have unexpected consequences. Corn snakes pose a threat to native Caribbean wildlife as they feed on small rodents, lizards and birds.

Are corn snakes only invasive or also useful?

Although some people see corn snakes as a threat, farmers are usually happy when they see one on their land. Corn snakes help to control rodent populations. Rats and mice can spread diseases and cause great damage to crop. Farmers can hire a pest controller or use a cat as a rat hunter, but a Corn snake does the job for free and efficiently. Being carnivorous and feeding on rodents, lizards, birds, eggs and the like, Corn snakes play an important role in agriculture. They are useful exterminators in the local ecosystem.

Who is bigger - a male Corn snake or a female Corn snake?

There are no gender differences. When Corn snakes hatch, they are usually between 20 and 30 centimetres long. As adults, corn snakes can reach a length of 60 to 180 centimetres. This is true for both males and females.

By Kapa65 Karsten Paulick

Legal Notice

This book is protected by copyright. Reproduction by third parties is prohibited. Use or distribution by unauthorised third parties in any printed, audiovisual, audio or other media is prohibited. All rights remain solely with the author.

Author: Alina Daria Djavidrad

Contact: Wahlerstraße 1, 40472 Düsseldorf, Germany.

© 2023 Alina Daria Djavidrad

1st edition (2023)

Dear Readers 🖤

For independent authors, product reviews are the foundation of a book's success. That is why we depend on your reviews.

This helps not only the authors, but of course also future readers and especially the animals!

Therefore, I should be grateful for a little review on this book. Thank you so much for your support! 😊

I wish you all the best, much joy with your pets and stay healthy!

Room for Notes

Printed in Great Britain
by Amazon

41609826R00040